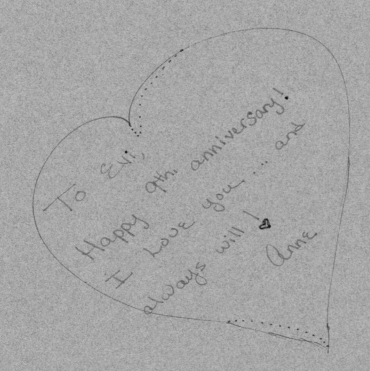

To Evi,
Happy 9th anniversary!
I love you ... and
always will !
Anne

Sequoias

Michael George

Designed by Rita Marshall
with the help of Thomas Lawton

Published in 1993 by Creative Editions
123 South Broad Street
Mankato, Minnesota 56001

Creative Editions is an imprint of
Creative Education, Inc. This title is
published as a joint effort between
Creative Education, Inc. and American
Education Publishing.

Photography by Frank Balthis,
Gary Braasch, Carr Clifton,
Ric Ergenbright, Mark Gibson,
Light Images, Galen Rowell,
Trygve Steen, Larry Ulrich,
and Visuals Unlimited

Library of Congress
Cataloging-in-Publication Data

George, Michael, 1964–
Sequoias / by Michael George.
Summary: Examines the physical
characteristics, growth patterns, and
longevity of the redwood and giant
sequoia and discusses how they resemble
and differ from each other.
ISBN 1-56846-055-4
1. Giant sequoia—Juvenile literature.
2. Redwood—Juvenile literature.
[1. Redwood. 2. Giant sequoia.]
I. Title.   91-3696
QK494.5.T3G46   1991
585'.2—dc20

In Memory of
GEORGE R. PETERSON, SR.

7

Trees of all shapes, sizes, and colors dot the landscape of our globe. Many of us pass hundreds of trees each day, but in the hurry and confusion of our lives, few of us take notice of their existence. Yet among the Earth's trees there stands a giant: the *Sequoias*. Unique among trees, sequoias demand our attention and seldom go unnoticed.

Rhododendrons bloom in a grove of redwood trees.

Unlike other trees, sequoias are so huge that they seem to lack the normal features of a trunk, branches, and leaves. Instead, they appear to be towering pillars resting on immense, immovable foundations. Some sequoias stretch to heights of over three hundred and fifty feet, and many are over thirty feet wide. The tremendous weight of a sequoia compresses the tree's foundation, cementing it to the Earth. Bulging muscles of wood and bark, stiffened and strained, support the massive tree. Even during the most violent storms, the sequoias barely sway. They seem almost too massive, too permanent, too silent to be alive.

Sequoia National Park, California.

In a *Sequoia Grove,* the space above your head is open and uncluttered; the lowest branches of the trees may be one hundred feet above the ground. Above the lowest heavy limbs is a covering of needles and cones that creates an appearance of twilight on the forest floor. The fairytale-like atmosphere is accentuated by rays of sunshine that beam through the distant canopy.

❧

Sequoias have existed on Earth for millions of years. Ancestors of the sequoias existed during the time of the dinosaur, nearly 200 million years ago. At one time, there were over thirty kinds of sequoias growing in Asia, Europe, Greenland, and North America. Over the ages, the Earth's climate has changed and most of the sequoias have died out. Today, only two kinds of sequoias survive: the redwood and the giant sequoia.

Sunlight filters through the sequoias.

Of the two surviving types of sequoias, *Redwoods* are by far the tallest. In fact, redwoods are the tallest trees in the world. The tallest standing redwood, called *The Founders' Tree*, is located on the famous Redwood Highway in northern California. The Founders' Tree, surrounded by neighbors that range from 350 to 360 feet tall, stretches to a height of 367 feet. Lying on its side, the Founders' Tree would dwarf the length of a football field.

The world's tallest trees.

15

Although the redwood is the tallest tree in the world, it is not the largest in total weight. That honor goes to the other surviving variety of sequoia, the *Giant Sequoia*. The best-known giant sequoia is the one called *General Sherman* in Sequoia National Park. Although lightning severed the uppermost part of the tree centuries ago, General Sherman is estimated to weigh nearly five million pounds, far more than any other living tree. In fact, at five million pounds, General Sherman is the most massive living thing on Earth.

Page 14: The tree known as General Grant.
Page 15: Giant sequoias in Yosemite National Park.

17

Even if their appearances were not distinctive, it would be hard to confuse a redwood and a giant sequoia because the two trees grow in widely separated locations. Redwoods thrive in areas that receive fifty inches of rain every year, in addition to a soaking fog every night. They also prefer hot days, cool nights, and infrequent winter frosts. Rarely are they found more than fifty miles from the ocean. Dependent on these particular conditions, redwoods grow only in a limited area in northern California, near the Pacific coast.

Redwoods in the mist.

Giant sequoias, on the other hand, prefer cool, high altitudes between five and eight thousand feet. They are found exclusively in the Sierra Nevada, a mountain range in California, where they rely on deep winter snows for much of their water. Residing at such high altitudes, giant sequoias must cling to rocks and sand. Unable to plunge deep beneath the surface, the roots of a giant sequoia may venture one hundred feet from the trunk in search of water and nutrients.

Sequoias in the snow.

Besides differing in size and habitat, redwoods and giant sequoias also are dissimilar in their methods of reproduction. Redwoods do not grow well from seed. The cones are small and produce seeds that frequently are infertile. However, redwoods have surprisingly potent wood. When a redwood is damaged by man or nature, shoots sprout from the fallen logs or cut stumps. Slowly, gradually, the tree begins its long journey back toward the sky. Redwoods also reproduce from knotty growths called burls. *Burls* grow on the trunks of redwoods and produce an abundance of redwood treelets every year.

A redwood's burls.
Inset: Sprouting redwoods.

Unlike redwoods, giant sequoias do not reproduce from burls or shoots. Instead, they rely solely on seeds for reproduction. Seeds develop in cones located high in the trees; normally, their development takes twenty years. After the seeds have matured, the cones are torn from the tree by a strong wind or heavy snow.

❧

Even after falling hundreds of feet to the forest floor below, the seeds of a giant sequoia are not released from the protective cone. Giant sequoias rely on fire, insects, or squirrels to destroy the cone and disperse the seeds that are contained inside. Of the one hundred and fifty to two hundred seeds in a cone, only twenty to thirty are fertile. And of these twenty or thirty fertile seeds, only a few are lucky enough to sprout. They require a soil rich in minerals and plenty of sunshine, conditions that are hard to come by in a forest of giant sequoias.

Page 22: Redwood cones.
Page 23: A fire at Yosemite.

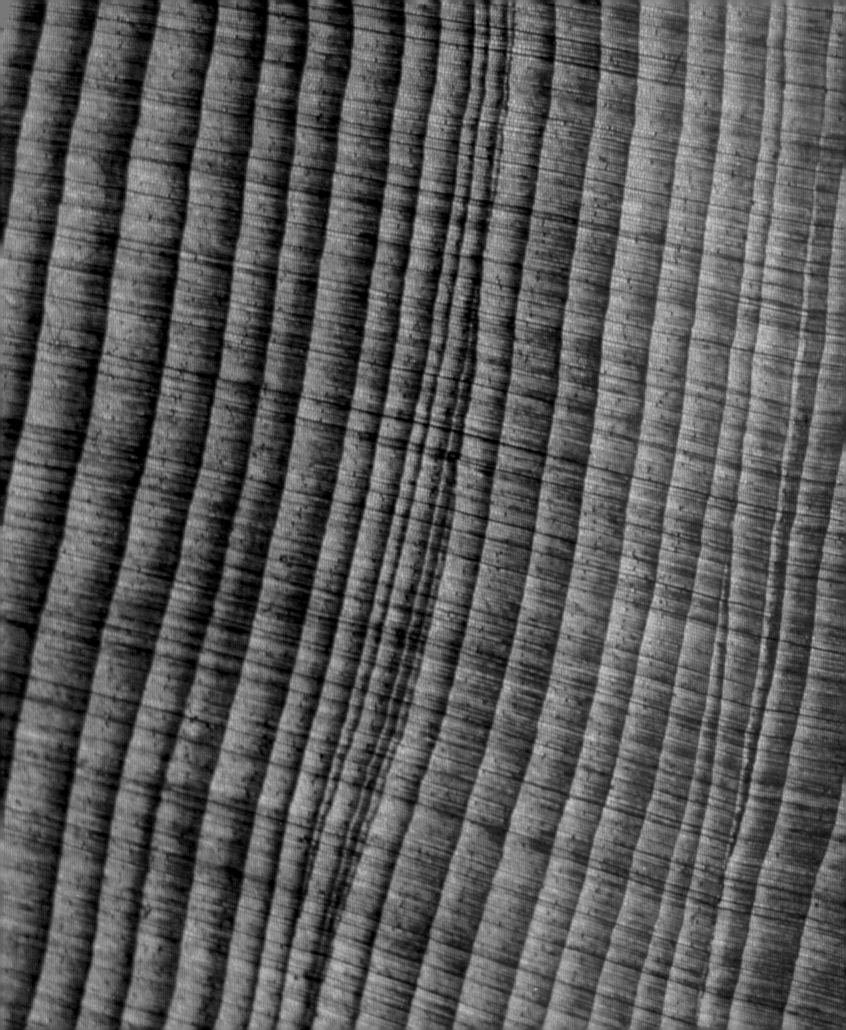

Though the redwood and giant sequoia differ in size, habitat, and method of reproduction, they also share many similarities. One similarity is the length of their lives.

❧

In order to determine the age of any tree, a forester must somehow see inside the tree. One way to do this is to cut down the tree. When a tree is cut down, a pattern of *Rings* can be seen on the remaining stump. Each ring represents how much the tree trunk grew in a year. By counting the number of these growth rings, a forester can easily determine the age of the tree.

The growth rings of a redwood tree.
Inset: Needles on the forest floor.

However, foresters do not want to cut down a tree merely to determine its age. Instead, a forester can insert a long tube deep into the tree's trunk. When the tube is removed, it contains a long piece of the tree's wood. This piece of wood, called a *Core Sample*, shows the alternating light and dark bands of the tree's growth rings. By counting these bands, a forester can accurately determine the age of a tree.

It takes a long time for a forester to count the growth rings of a sequoia core sample. Samples of living sequoias reveal that many are between three and four thousand years old. These trees survived the fall of the Roman Empire, existed at the time of Christ, and, it is hoped, will outlive the atomic age. They have stood for centuries, indifferent to the drastic changes that have taken place in human society. Compared to the lives of the sequoias, our lives are mere seconds in the expanse of time.

A fire-scarred giant sequoia.

One reason sequoias live so long is because they are fire-resistant. Unlike other trees, sequoias do not contain highly flammable pitch and resin. In addition, sequoias have soft, spongy bark that protects the trees' inner heartwood from flames. The bark of mature trees, textured with long, deep creases, reaches thicknesses of up to two feet. Even if a violent fire manages to burn through the protective bark, the wood contains much water, making it difficult to ignite.

The Telescope Tree in Yosemite National Park illustrates the sequoias' ability to survive a serious fire. In 1862, a ferocious fire burned through the protective bark and even damaged the heartwood of the Telescope Tree. Today, well over a hundred years later, the Telescope Tree is still alive. Because of the fire, you can now look up through its trunk and see the blue sky, as if the tree were a giant, living telescope.

Lichens grow on the thick bark of the sequoia.
Inset: The still-living Chimney Tree, Prairie Creek State Park.

Another reason sequoias are able to live so long is because they produce a substance called *Tannin*. Tannin helps protect the giant trees against insect damage, disease, and decay, which are the primary causes of death for most other trees.

Protected against fire, insects, and disease, sequoias face few natural threats. However, the sequoias' root systems do not always provide adequate support for their massive trunks. As a result, being toppled by strong winds is often the cause of a sequoia's death.

A fallen giant.

Unfortunately, humankind poses more of a threat to the sequoias than does nature. Although Indians used the wood of the sequoias for hundreds of years, the giant trees went undiscovered by white settlers in California until the mid-1800s. In 1852 a man by the name of A. T. Dowd was tracking a grizzly bear when he came across a towering sequoia. Astonished by the tree's immense size, Dowd forgot about the bear and rushed back to camp, excited to tell his friends he had discovered the tallest tree in the world. To his disappointment, no one believed his claim.

Frustrated, Dowd invented a new story about a giant grizzly bear. This time he was able to lure the miners to the massive sequoia. When they came upon the tree, they were astonished by its tremendous size. News of the awesome tree, and the many others like it, spread quickly to San Francisco and the east.

Page 32: Colorful fungi in a redwood forest.
Page 33: The gnarled trunk of a giant sequoia.

As quickly as the sequoias became famous, lumber companies began cutting them down. Fortunately, the chain saw had not yet replaced the hand ax. A lumberjack chopping at a sequoia with a hand ax is like a woodpecker banging at an oak with its beak. Cutting down the sequoias with a hand saw was not much easier. The work was difficult and the progress slow.

Moro Rock at Sequoia National Park.
Inset: Sequoias fallen among the ferns.

Unfortunately, lumber companies quickly invented more efficient methods for toppling the sequoias. One way lumberjacks brought the trees down was by drilling holes in the trees' trunks. Weakened by the holes, the trees were blown over by strong winds. Lumberjacks also used dynamite to blow the trees off their foundations. This practice required less time and effort, but the explosion splintered much of the wood, making it useless. Despite all the dangers and difficulties, by 1917 many sequoias along the California coast had been leveled.

Mountain dogwood and giant sequoias.

Finally people began to recognize the importance of protecting the magnificent sequoias. In 1920 citizens concerned about the survival of the sequoias formed the *Save-the-Redwoods* League. This group helped prevent the ultimate destruction of the towering trees. Over the years, members gained protection for numerous sequoia groves throughout the state of California. The majority of sequoias are now within the boundaries of California's national parks, where they are protected against lumbering. Today, the sequoias face no immediate threat of extinction.

Sequoias are protected from logging in California's national parks.

Fortunately, the majestic *Sequoias* were saved from human destruction, for the redwood and the giant sequoia represent something unique on the face of the Earth. The awe we feel toward the sequoia cannot be expressed in diameters, heights, and ages; it can be felt only when we trespass into their realm. Entering a grove of sequoias, one steps softly and speaks in a whisper. There is no sense of time, no wind, and no sound. A visit to the sequoias is a moving, spiritual experience that can be had nowhere else on Earth.

The timeless majesty of a redwood grove.